together

 **lovin touch**

dick summer

photography:
steve hansen

design:
marghi bean

published by subway productions, inc.
twelve irving street, framingham, mass. 01701

First printing - August 1971

ISBN : 0-912270-02-0

Printed in United States of America

foreword

While you read this book,
We share a closeness that grows from touching a real love.

If you give this book to someone else...
Then we are three...
Until the two of you
Are one.

Dick Summers

lovin touch I

walls
sky sultan
who are you?
in the chill time of dawn
signals
small world
waking
remember being alone?
cycles
winter
instead you have me
spring

lovin touch II

trust me
winter of the world
getting to know you
christmas warm
honey
lady ice and eve
walking
your innocence
closer
tears
naked eyes
the thin line
we take each other too much for granted
quiet

walls

Walls run all around our lives;
Back yard fences that hide drying laundry
And swimming pools,
And mirror lens sunglasses that hide
Our eyes and thoughts.
Thin, polite smiles are walls
Hiding sneers.
And when hair is sprayed stiff enough,
It keeps playful fingers
And gentle breezes out.

And there are walls you can't see.
Like the blank silences
Where gentle words should be,
And the space between single beds.
There are even walls when people kiss.
When she hugs herself instead of him,
Forcing her elbows up between them,
Not letting her softness spread...warm...on his chest.
And does he call that kissing her?
He seems to enjoy hurting her mouth.

I've met people who do without walls.
Friends who welcome me to kitchens moist with cooking
Instead of formal living rooms.
Some who flip quarters to see who buys the beer,
But would give me every cent they had if I needed it.
A few who listen when I talk,
And laugh with me when I'm happy,
And cry with me when I fail.
I even have friends,
One or two,
Who really want me to succeed.

And...
I have
You.

Now we are two candles feeding one flame.
But first we were good friends.
The change was on the night of a day that left me crumpled
Like an old raincoat carelessly tossed on a bed.
You knew.
And you came.

Because you are my friend,
You came without stopping
To straighten your seams,
Or fix your hair,
Or do makeup repair.
And so you came with bare legs,
And wind fresh hair,
And soft, hurt eyes.

The momentum of your coming so fast
Took you across a wall I didn't even know was there.
You came so close I touched your dress.
At first, inside,
It was like a squirrel nibbling peanuts
From the crease of my palm.
But when you trembled
As my fingers touched your hair,
And sat slowly,
All soft, like folding fur,
I was running naked into warm ocean surf.

But I remember bending down
To kiss your open lips,
And seeing your left shoulder
Touch your ear.
You were all lips that night.
And everywhere I touched you,
You kissed my fingertips.
I heard my voice say, "I love you."

My sweet lady, those words
Still rub against my teeth and lips
As smooth and gentle as your skin.
I love you.
But I am told I love you too much.
I love you in this way the world calls outrageous.
I will not stop.
And I will do what must be done
To protect you.

Must I build walls?

sky sultan

Remember?
We agreed.
It was a savage,
Purple robed,
Golden cloud sultan,
Astride three black thunder stallions.
He brandished
The curved silver scimitar
Of the new moon
Over his ruby turban...
And giving a north-east shriek,
Smashed through the great bronze shield
That protects heaven
From earth's day view.

Then,
Day's murder done,
We watched the empty sky sultan
Unwind...
His tumbling sword splattering
Into a mist of silent midnight silver
Against sandy cliffs...
Tinseling pines...
Mirroring your shadow,
In the fine wet sand.

Remember the beach music?
Guitars and bongos,
Filtering through the silk gauze
Of gentle summer air.
Suntanned voices,
Shimmering over driftwood bonfires.
The bass surf percussion
Pumping caves in clouds...
Filling the empty dipper.

And out past the breakers a little...
Holding you very close,
Because you don't swim well,
Your modest straps burning my wet chest,
A new kiss still very fresh on your lips,
My reward for saving you from stepping
On an imaginary crab.
Remember my right arm crushing your shoulders,
My left holding your knees bent high over the surf?

And then I lunged and ran,
Carrying you,
Until I tripped on a deserted
Sand castle turret.
You laughed as we fell in a tumble
On an old woolen blanket
On the sand.

We lay side by side for a long time,
Letting the sun bake the salt
From the sea drops
On our arms,
And backs,
And legs.

I guess that seagull's voice
Wasn't like so much tearing
Sheet metal.
But he zippered across the beach
Only eight feet high
When he shrieked.

And my ears had just devoured
Your gentle "thank you"
For the mother-of-pearl shell
That I found for you
By the rocks.

Your eyes were still half full
Of your quick afternoon nap.
Your face like a little girl's...
Innocent and lovely.
The fine dusting of sand
The sea breeze gave you
Was like new kitten fur.

I poured trickles of love words
Down the nape of your neck.
And you shivered...
Not from any chill.

But that was long ago.
And it was so much more
Than people can really love.
I guess that Sky Sultan we saw
Was a sorcerer,
And the magic will never happen
Again.

Except,
Perhaps,
Tonight.
Because tonight,
The new moon is a brandishing scimitar.
And thunder stallions ride.
And silent midnight silver
Is on the world.

who are you?

Who are you?

I don't mean your name.
That's just some words
Your parents gave you.
I mean, who are you?

What are you?
I don't mean your job.
Others do the same work as you.
Some of them even better than you.
But what are you?

Until you find out
Who and what you are,
You get pushed around
Into lumpy crowds.
And if you resist,
You get sent alone
Down long dark hallways
With red lit signs
Marked EXIT,
All pointing in different directions
In echoing sky scrapers
With self service elevators.

I found the outline of myself
By touching against you.

I don't know why
You touched me back
Instead of all the other men
Who have reached out for you.
But somehow,
Whatever I am
Touched you.
I knew it when you caught me
Staring at your legs.

Your eyes slid
All the way up
My line of sight
To my eyes,
And you spent
What seemed like an hour
Softening there.

I'm glad I couldn't help looking.
It's your walk.
It makes a butterfly
Of the hem of your dress
Against your legs,
And I am attracted to
Such soft and supple things.

I saw myself living,
For the first time
In your eyes.
And ever since then,
I've been able to walk
Down a city block
Full of strangers,
And grin, and sing, and smile,
Just because I feel good,
And I never even feel foolish anymore.

Thank you.

Whoever you are.

in the chill time of dawn

In the chill time of dawn,
While the last black breeze
Dusts her hills with powder snow,
She turns herself,
Our loving earth,
Till the sun touches
Through her black lace cloud.
His first burst
Of long warm light
Arouses her quick cry.
And that wakes the day.

In the chill time of dawn,
When the earth
First feels the touching sun,
And wraps her trees and waves
Around his neck
So he can kiss her
Deep and giant-full,
Her quick cry
Rouses each living thing.
Oceans and volcanoes are her voice.

But, in the chill time of dawn,
You
Are a nylon voiced guitar
Chording with me...
Tumble-warm and soft.

There's a night veil of hair
Spun across your face.
But my lips find your lips
All naked, warm, and real.
Crests of woman,
Still evening soft and moist,
Curling next to me
All velvet voiced.
Your hair is fine and soft dark brown
Here around my hands,
And on my face.

And so it is so many times at dawn.
But it's always like the first time
When I fastened a pendant chain
Around your neck.
And in the tingling excitement
Of being so close with you,
I could feel the roundness
Of each strand of your hair
Brush against my fingernails.
And that fingertip touch
Chilled my elbow
Deep inside.
Like when I was little,
And my father lifted me high enough
So that by straining
As tall as I could,
My fingernails grazed
The white plaster ceiling.

Little boys like to play at giant.
So do grown up men.

And in the chill time of dawn,
You make me feel tall and strong.
So I'll sweep my hand
Round the earth's rim,
And scoop the first flakes of light
Into my palm.
Then twirling them between my hands
Into a shining string,
I'll tie it round your finger,
And you'll wear it
For a gentle, loving, ring.
And I will kiss your hands warm,
In the chill time of dawn.

signals

Signals snap us on and off.
They send us scurrying across streets
And start a football team in motion.
They stop taxi cabs
And cut a broadcast off the air.

We even obey signals
That can't be explained.
Just touching glances with a stranger
Walking toward you on the street
Guides you both
So that you pass without colliding.
And haven't you choked
On the lumpy pause in a conversation
That comes when you've asked an indiscreet question?
And haven't you seen someone cross his legs
And wiggle his foot
When you've stayed a little too long?

Our lives roll along on thousands of these
Tiny signal wheels.
We can usually steer them
So they take us pretty much where we thought we'd go.
But sometimes, one turns suddenly
In an unexpected direction.

Like when your one tiny signal
Turned my life completely around.

All you did was stand quietly behind me.

But you stood an inch closer than you had to.
I knew you were there
Before I saw or heard you.
You know how your skin tickles
Just before a teasing finger
Really touches?

That's how I felt
Your sleek legs and frilly lace blouse
At the back of my neck.
And your voice
Was one degree warmer than it had to be
When you said hello.
When I turned to face you, you looked up
And smiled.

You were almost touching my chest.
Your perfume,
Warmed by our standing so close,
Rose through your hair to my face.
And tiny red rocks, with sharp points
Went tumbling all over
The edges of my skin.

Signals?
I was a neon sign, I guess.

Your laugh was like spring water
Splashing on moss covered stones.

I had to scoop you up into my arms
And twirl you around
All kicking and laughing
And holding on tight as you whirled,
Like some soft pink baby seal
Wriggling warm in the sunlight,
Playing and licking at my face.

Getting to know you,
Was like running barefoot
Through all my softest dreams.
You learned to scratch my back
Just hard enough
And at exactly the right speed and angle.
And you loved to stretch
And smile when I kissed your back
From shoulder to shoulder
Exactly where your hair tips
Touch your skin.
And the pink roundings of your shoulders
Were like baby cheeks in my hands.

We played, and we worked, and laughed,
Over zippers and things.
I still think you wear them behind
To be more helpless
And gently dependent on me.

And we learned how it feels to feel nothing
Because we cried more than we could
Over Kennedy, Kennedy and King.

Our signals flew fast,
Much faster than words.
Till in time, words just got in our lips way.
Till today.

Our smiles wouldn't touch today.
Our signals are here, but they're not together.
They're like roads to the beach
That seem out of place in the winter.
And why do I feel you peeling apart
At the words to some song
That means nothing to me.

My lady,
I just saw my face looking back from your eyes.
It was never that shade there before.
And you've just clicked the locket
I won for you last July.
Have you noticed the sound?
It's like an automatic record changer
That just played the last record
In the stack,
And switched itself
Off.

small world

It's such a small world
And there are so many people on it.
In a little while
There won't be room to lie down.

It's such a small world,
And with so many people on it
We're almost out of air, and water
And even time and space enough to think.

Rush hour crowds bruise shoulders
In a hating hurry to get home
To houses full of strangers...
People, familied together,
But never touching.

How can there be
So many strangers,
Never touching...
Apart and alone...
When there are such crowds
On this very small world.

Come, my lovely lady,
Lie down...
Touch with me
While there is still room,
While there is still time.

Breathe deep, fresh and pure...
Love like a young earth
Quaking with new life under me.

Be my small world.

waking

My head is attached
To our alarm clock
Even while the rest of me
Sleeps
Wrapped around you
From loving through the night.

So this morning
At the pre-set time
My head tried to drag us apart.
But my fingers were tangled
In your hair,
And my legs were trapped
Between your thighs.

My head buzzed with
"You have bills to pay
And things to buy."

Then you pressed your breast
Against my chest
And turned my mind off.

remember being alone?

Remember when you were alone?
It isn't quite the same
As being lonely, is it.
Alone means empty.
But alone is hungry.
So when you're alone
You're always hoping
Someone will come
To fill up your empty space
Until it just disappears.

I know you haven't felt alone
For a long time.
The lonely got you,
Didn't it.

Lonely chews deeper into a woman
Than it can into a man.
A man can hide from himself...
Behind football games on TV,
A harder grind at work,
Even polishing his car...
So his whole world can marvel
At him standing
And shining.
Five blocks away.
But a woman is mostly
A feeling,
Caring
Mink coat pocket.
She's made that way
To thaw a frostbitten man.

In fact, that's why she cries...
If she didn't
Her tears would freeze hard
Inside her.
And she needs to be soft enough
To stretch as her man fills her.
And he must have her to fill.
Or he'd drown in himself.

But you were warming a thief
Inside you
And he escaped
With your heart still tightly wrapped around him.

I know I can't touch your heart
Right now,
Because you don't own it anymore.
But if you'd try
You could grow
Another one, you know.
It would be completely different
From your old one.
You might not even recognize
How it would feel.

Brand new hearts feed on
Baby laughs,
Soft Christmas Eve snows,
And old lovers
Still holding hands.

Take a chance...
Let me bring you these.
And let me keep you young and warm
With new daisies for your hair,
Gentle touchings on your face,
And barefoot laughing walks
On the grass
In warm summer rain.

Then don't be surprised
As your new heart grows
If you feel something missing
Inside you again.
It won't be the same as before,
But at least you'll have
Some space inside
Where you can feel
Soft and empty again.

Maybe you'll even have
Room enough for me.

cycles

Is three a.m. very early,
Or is it very late?
It's the end of a nightclub singer's day,
But the beginning of the milkman's.
On the clock it's early morning,
But there's no real change if we call it
Very late at night.
As long as one day dies,
The next begins.

A seed drowns in water,
Suffocates in warm crushing earth,
Rots and dies,
So a blade of grass can chop away
At winter's ice.

But how can crumbling death
Play tag with the sun,
And touch life to spring?
Unless it doesn't really change life
To call it death.

I have life as a man,
You as a woman.
And how is that,
When life is like God,
Neither male nor female,
...but both.
Especially since it's only by being
Man and woman
That we can produce another life,
And fully feel our own.

"Man" and "Woman"
Must mean more than
Male and female.

I was born male.
And so when I learned to walk,
I wanted to run;
When I ran, I tried to jump...
Higher, and faster
Than others my own age
And kind.
I tumbled,
Swam,
Wrestled,
Lifted,
Raced,
And bragged.
I wanted to be like
A sweating, strutting, midnight,
Steam diesel
Locomotive,
Pounding freight into a mountain tunnel.

I wanted to plunge into life
Swinging a long, hard,
Double handed sword...

Until I saw you,
Sitting and watching.
You were just brushing your hair,
And warming inside your smile.

You taught me that hair is for nose tips,
Smiles are for touching lips,
And warmth is for man and woman together.

I don't know how you came to be there so close to my life...
Just sitting,
Smiling,
Warming,
And brushing your hair.
But I think you always knew
That you would be the sheath for my sword.

When I felt the brushed sparks
From your hair
Split on my arm,
You made me feel your need
To curl your summer moist,
Woman softness
Around me.

You said I was gentle,
But my finger
Triggered bells and electric music
All along the hollow
Of your back.
Gentle?
Was I gentle?

I thought I had to make myself hard
To be a man.

You'd have seen my surprise,
But your eyes were closed over your smile.
And your head was making small circles
On my shoulder.
And you were saying that for the first time,
You,
Were a woman.

We're so different you and I.
As different as the two opposite parts
Of the same life.

winter

The icy midnight air makes ground glass of the late winter sky.
The earth is a purple cave behind the Niagara of the Milky Way.
A DC-9's rumble echoes in the canyon etched by its own vapor trail,
A shimmering silver chalice toasting the universe
With the champagne of man himself.
After a winter of snow,
This night pours from the dipper...
Clean, clear, and cold.
It's a traveling night...
The kind of night that drives some men's minds
To send Apollo looking back over the shoulder of the moon
At our emerald earth.

I have a journey planned too...a much simpler one.
I've traveled it a thousand times.
But the thought of discovering you again at its end,
Jabs an edge of black cold air deeper inside my lungs than I expected.
And so I go crashing through the crisp cold,
Last week's still frozen sleet snapping under my tearing tires.
Past boarded windows
And desperate doorway dark that seeps into the yellow sponge
Of the street light...
Through smudged fingers of city air peeling the green paint
Off a brick wall
...the red stop light sentinels senselessly guarding the right of way
For empty streets between us...
Stopping my car
And opening my eyes and ears to the uncaged prowlings of the night.

The windmill steps of a middle-aged man who has had one too many
Trying to forget
...and in his sagging eyes the despair of stubborn memories.
From an all-night joint,
The blue light sandpaper laughter of a night of conquest.
At one dim corner the faint but distinct sound
Of brushing nylon,
Cut into lengths by snapping high heels.
A solitary figure on a bridge...
Is that a cigarette or a pencil in his hand?

Crazy word license plates shining under salt-grimed bumpers
...G-I-A-N-T,
Driven by a darkly bearded man
With steel eyes looking into my rearview mirror.
An expensive foreign limousine tagged
MOGUL,
Motor running by a curb.
A happy
SKI-WEE
With ski rack on the back,
Looking like a weather radar antenna
Searching for more snow.

Forty red lights screaming in the wake of a truck on a crossroad
...the compressed air bell of an all-night gas station
...and those two people kissing happily.
Right in the middle of the street.
That's worth a big crazy smile inside.

She looked nothing like you...
But she made me remember the first time you kissed me back...
How the sun turned new blue
When I felt you pressing back against me
...and red raindrops pounded on my ears.

I wrapped strands of your smooth hair
Gently between my thumb and forefinger,
Tracing down your cheek
And into the valley between your chin and your lip.
The intimate excitement of you
Tingled under the arches of my feet
Like scuffing barefoot
Across a deep pile rough wool carpet.
Gently rising and swelling electric rivers
Flowed between us,
Tempting the woman deep in you to the edges of your mouth
For me to taste.

You said I made you feel
Like popcorn in the sun
...and we laughed
Because it was night
And we were saying things
That only two people in love may say
When it's very late.

Now, here in our front yard,
In the moonlit snow,
A small pine tree stands quietly...
Like a child in her nightgown.

And...in this room
...We
Give birth
To spring.

instead you have me

You're lovely,
Sweetheart.
You should have
A handsome prince
Or a famous movie star
For a lover.
Or at least
The first man
To land on Mars.
Instead,
You have me.

You don't need mirrors
To see that you're beautiful.
Every man you meet
Stumbles
All over his knuckles
Trying to get
Close to you.
You could take your pick
Of Paul Newmans
Or harvest
A bumper crop
Of Joe Namaths.
Instead,
You have me.

I'm not helpless
But I'm no hero.
The world and I
Were just about even.
And that was good enough
For me.
Until I caught you
Talking about how proud
You are
Of who and what I am.
Ever since then,
I want to be more than
"Just good enough."

I think
The wanting to be
Is even more important
Than what I really am.
Most of the good
In this world
Is in the wanting.

Isn't Christmas Eve
More exciting
Than Christmas Day?
And if it is,
Then sea shells
From the beach
Where I first kissed
Your naked legs
Are more valuable
Than pearls
From a gold-plated
Jewelry store...
And carefully peeled
Orange sections
Held up to
Sunday's sunrise
Praise God better
Than stained glass windows.

We hold very private services
Lying close enough together
To admire all of God's morning
Through the same
Orange slice.

We administer
To each other
Our bodies' holy oils...
Still hot
From boiling inside
Our love.

I annoint you,
The way a minute hand
Moves around a clock.
Slowly,
Thoroughly,
Until the end of the hour
Trips the alarm,
And we plunge together
Startled,
Legs kicking...
Running for balance,
Flying to the floor
Of a newly
Whirling world.
Then...
You are even lovelier
In sleep.

Sweetheart,
You should wake
Beside a handsome prince
Or a famous movie star,
Or at least the first man
To land on Mars.
But instead,
You have me.
If you'll roll over
You'll stop distracting me
So much,
And I'll scratch your back
And legs
Gently,
With my chin,
Before I shave.

spring

Spring doesn't descend from heaven;
It is simply our lovely earth.
Wakened from the numbing anesthesia of winter
By the prodding of newly returned birds
In search of food.
She stretches sleepily,
Cracking the ice
At the base of her mountains
And in her deep river beds.
She rolls over
Inside her dull gray and dirty white blanket,
Crying April tears for the tiny creatures
Huddled hungry there with her.

Then noticing more and more
Of Father Sun's attention,
She blushes light green
And bright yellow,
Slips into a honeysuckle halter
And new grass skirt,
Lets the blue jays and butterflys
Rearrange her air,
And with a spray of fresh forsythia perfume,
She surrenders her warm wet fertility
To the strong new sun.

You taste different in the spring,
When your lips are first tinted by the orange sun.
Your neck feels young and smooth
On the first day you fling your heavy woolen scarf aside.
Even though your hair still has traces of the scent
Of winter's last pine fire,
The sun has already streaked lovely light fingers in your curls,
And they seem to try to hold my hands against your neck.

Your words are thoughts brushed on air,
Air that is fresh from a purple color thunder bath.
Air that I envy, because you breathe it so hungrily inside you.
But when I wet my finger to test the wind's direction,
To fly our yellow kite, you frown,
And say I shouldn't kiss the earth's breath, but just your own.
And then smiling, you nip at my finger tip
With your soft lips.
I try to joke, telling you that now
I've branded my fingerprint on your tongue.
But instead of laughing, you just press closer to me,
Your fresh fullness straining against the boundaries
Of your pretty pink cotton dress.
The earth feels soft and moist in spring,
And you are spring in my arms.

the lovin touch

What does that TV newscaster write
On his papers
When the camera stays on him
After he's flashed his goodnight smile?

Probably, "Eat your heart out Walter Cronkite,"
Or "Nixon can't stand Pat,"
Or even "Remember to get the car washed."

Maybe he'd be writing our names
If he knew we broke the world's touching record
Right in front of him tonight.

I'm proud of us.

I don't know if I've ever seen you
So relaxed and satisfied.
Well, you should be.
We loved long and strong.

And now the flicking gray tongue
Of his television picture
Licks up your legs and hips
Tasting your warm softnesses
On its way to playing in your hair.

It's hard to see the rest of you.
You're half embedded in the sheets.
Well, I won't worry about losing you in there
As long as your hand is still folded
Inside mine.

That's our special hand-made-connection.
It gets us strange looks at parties,
In stores and at concerts.
Imagine!
A grown up man and woman holding hands.

The world should know how warm
Two hands in one coat pocket feel
On a cold night,
Or how a cool and gentle hand can soothe
All the anger from a fist.

But I'm glad no one can overhear
Our long, private
Finger - conversations.
We sometimes burst out laughing because of them
And they sometimes make your eyes
Suddenly go soft and wanting
Even though nobody has said a word.

Right now, my fingers can still feel
How you look.

All of you.

And I'm sure that it wasn't
So you'd look different tonight
That you tied your hair back
With a red velvet ribbon.

You just didn't want anything,
Not even your own hair,
Between you
And my hands
Touching you past hungry loving,
Into sleep.

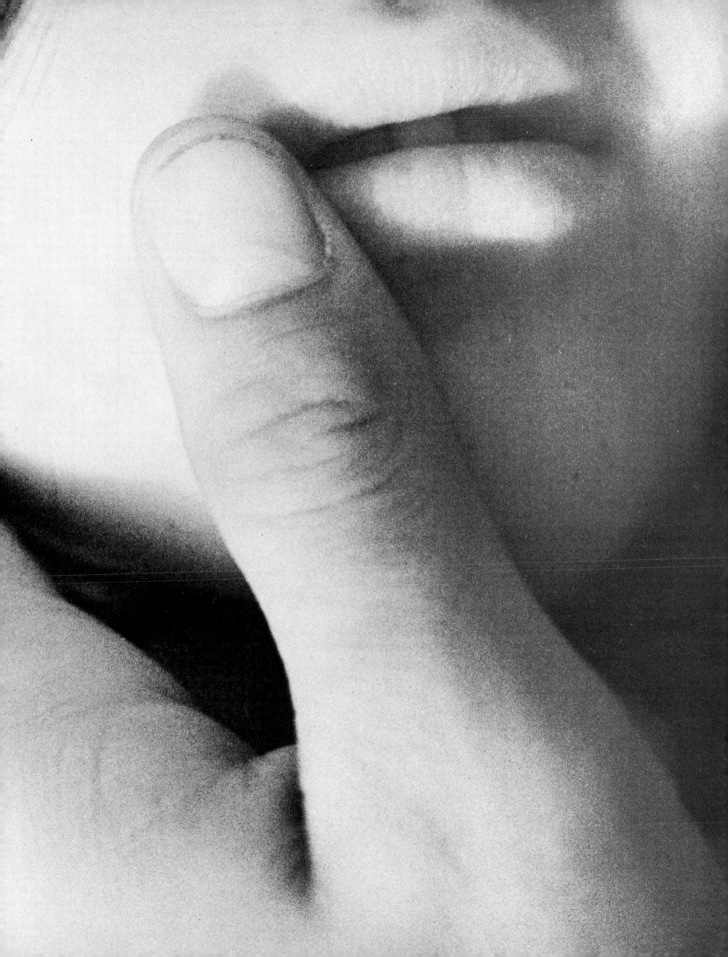

trust me

Trust me,
Always.
Believe I love you.
Wait for me to open doors,
And hold your coat for you.
Trust me to listen when you talk.
Even when your legs
Distract me from your words,
Your thoughts are important to me.
They are part of you.
And I want
All of you.

Trust me,
Always.
Believe I love you.
Forgive me when I forget
Our anniversary.
I never forget exactly how
Every one of our
"First times" felt,
And how you looked, and
What you said and did.

I remember you
Wearing the night
Shining through the small square window
Over the bed.
When you smiled and reached out your hand,
I knew for the first time
That loving me was more important
Than pride
To you.
And you
Trusted me
To love you.

But the polished night was less trusting .....
More cautious than you.
It covered the ridges your straps leave
On your shoulders and back,
And the small scar
That you use as an excuse
For never wearing a bikini.
But caution
Is like ridges and scars.
It has nothing to do with love.
And trusted fingers
Are more sensitive than eyes
To the personal sculptures
Of your warming skin.

You were so gently mine,
I didn't even think of hurts.
But I had time to wonder,
Waking before you
And watching the city dust
On the window pane
Turn gold
In the growing morning sun.

Your lips,
Sleeping on my shoulder,
Look like the kind of
Soft cherry-vanilla ice cream
That I like to carve into swirls
With my tongue.
Your lips sleep
Open a little ...

Even sleeping,
They're always asking
To be touched.

Please don't ever let another man
Touch your lips ...
Even with his fingers ...
Especially with his fingers .
My fingers find your lips
Like to be touched too much.
Trust me to touch them,
More than anyone else would.

And if I must be away
For awhile,
Look for me, in the love notes
That I've hidden
Around the kitchen,
And in the bedroom,
And under the couch.
And trust that I'll come back to you
As quickly as I can ...
To open doors for you,
And hold your coat ...
To touch you,
And listen when you talk.
And most of all,
Trust me to love you ...

And trust me
To trust you.
Always.

winter of the world

The proud god Apollo
Chops perforated footholds
As he climbs hand over hand
On his cardboard path to the Moon.

The tiny cutout pieces
Flutter back to Earth,
Smothering the upturned faces
Of his hungry subjects.
The new god "Computer"
Has decreed that Apollo
Must not fold, spindle, or mutilate
The thin, high road he rides
Or he will be cast into Hell,
And burned beyond recognition.

Meanwhile,
Mars, the hero god of war,
Outraged at Apollo's determined seduction
Of his cold and lovely sister the Moon,
Strikes lightning fire from the sky ...
And the growing drifts of cardboard
Computer card cutouts
Ignite all over the world.

War screams,
"The only way to save the burning human race
Is to extinguish the flames
With high pressure hosings of blood."
And the same red blood gushes from every man.

But Satan insists
"Look at his skin" ...
And laughs,
To see man
Turn on himself.

This is the winter of the world,
And as the white winter wolves howl,
Hate weaves an executioner's hood
For our Sun.

My room is solid with the frozen dark around me

But winter is born
On its own shortest day.
And in this world's longest night,
You opened my door ...
And a chiseled wedge of street light
Carved a curved space
For you to come in.

You were smiling ...
Shaking your rain drenched hair loose
From under your kerchief.

You wanted to surprise me
And the rain surprised you in return.

You were dripping wet,
But very full and warm in my arms.
There wasn't even lipstick between our lips
Because you know I'd rather taste you
Than paint.
But your lips feel red.
I think they ripen in the damp dark.

I hardly notice my fingers
Straighten and plunge into your hair,
Until your curls ride high on my knuckles.
And now there is a scent on my fingers
Playing in your hair.
It's a scent like spring brown earth
Under a misplaced April snow.

getting to know you

I'm getting to know you.
You're the pretty girl
Who still walks down the street
Eating an ice cream cone ...
Looking for pennies
Lucky side up ...
And stopping to smile
Into every passing baby carriage.

You thrill to shivers
At purple and gold sunsets.
And I think you really hear
The clear tinkling crystal
Of cold winter stars.

I'm getting to know you.
You're the young woman
Who flies her long brown hair
In summer thunderstorms ...
And dreams of Christmas
Every first time it snows.

Your eyes keep saying
I love you
Even when we're in a crowded bus
Or at concerts
Or at a ball game.

I'm getting to know you.
You're the soft, lovely lady
Who is always kind
To caterpillars and kittens.
You're afraid of mice,
But never want to see one trapped.

The ocean scares you too.
But you'll go out
Past where you can stand
If I'm there to hold you.
Last summer
You even said
You liked to feel
The water ripple
In your bathing suit.

I'm getting to know you.
You're the beautiful woman
Who laughs a lot with me
And with our friends ...
But you never laugh at me,
Or at a friend.

You cry at sad movies.
You cry at happy movies too.
Flowers please you
More than candy.
And when I bring you
Sheer little black frills
To wear at night,
You smile and close your eyes
Delicious for the feel
Of sheets and us.

I'm getting to know you.
You're my beautiful woman.

You don't hide from me ...
A soul ...
A spirit ...
Trapped somewhere
Inside your supple body.
Your body is not
A cage.

Your body is
The edge of you.

So it's not just to find
Sweet slidings of cool skin
That my hands and lips
Search your shoulders,
Your breasts,
Your thighs.

When we make love
Even your hands
And your forehead
Tremble from cool to warm.

All of you becomes a secret place
Where I can rub fires alive
Inside you ...
Loving fires
To melt all of you
Around me.

Even in our pouring heat,
You always stretch
And find some hidden fold
Of cool smooth skin
For me to warm ...
You're eager to help me ...
In getting to know you.

christmas warm

Bike bells,
Door bells,
Typewriter bells,
Fire bells,
Alarm clock bells ...
Bells trickle through the calendar,
Tinkling down the days
Almost ignored
Until November dies.

Then the school bells,
Timer bells,
Cash register bells,
All sing the sound of the season.
Big bells,
Baby bells,
Telephone bells ...
Telephone bells ...
They're the ones
That give a glisten
To the silver Christmas air

It was in an icicled outdoor telephone booth
With the door frozen open,
And a small snow drift in the coin return slot,
That I called to ask
If you wanted to go Christmas shopping.
You said yes,
In a voice
That curled around and into my ear
Moist and warm
From inside you.

It was like slowly pressing my foot
Into a warmed fur lined
Bedroom slipper.
That was the first time
I ever really enjoyed the bustle of shopping.

When we finished,
We stood in the brilliant cold
To watch the flashing Christmas tree lights
In the park.
Their reflections made
Candlelit
Stained glass windows
Of your eyes.

Right there,
In the swirl of gold wrapping paper
And red ribbon bows,
In the tumble of the hustling crowd ...
While your arms were trapped
Under the bundles of Christmas gifts
You'd just bought ...
I said "Merry Christmas"
And kissed you.
It took you by surprise,
And you flicked your eyelashes
Wide enough for me to look
At something that few women
Ever show a man.

For as long as it took my breath
To melt a snowflake
From your wind tangled hair,
You slipped out of the delicate black lace
Of feminine mystery.
Your eyes fed me
The full, round, warm
Honey
Of your most personal love.

I don't think it was
Just my breath that painted
Pink frost crystals
On your cheek.

You just closed your eyes,
And stood in an almost
Holy silence.

And that's how we rode home
That blizzard night.
The car's heater
Thawing the scent of green pine
From your fur collar.

We were so close
That I didn't even want the crunching
Of footsteps in the snow
Between us.
So I carried you from the car
To the house,
The flowered tops of your nylons
Blooming in the snow
Falling on my corduroy coat sleeve.
The jingle bells of my keys
Sounding the start of our first Christmas
Together.

After unbuttoning our snowy clothes
And rubbing our backs
On the black velvet dark
Of our quiet room,
You pressed the pink curves
Of your breasts and shoulders
To my chest.

You said
It made you
Warm.

honey

It hardly seems right
Calling you names like "Honey."
"Honey" doesn't seem special enough
For you.
Perhaps someday, I'll learn
Some better names to call you.
But you are a bit like honey, you know.

Until I gathered you carefully
Into my life,
You flew free
In golden sunlight.
Now you soften gently
In my mouth,
And on my fingers,
And you soothe the raw
Inside of me.

I call you beautiful, too.
Ever since I touched
The full curvings of your body.
How can you be so full,
And still tell me
That I've filled you
Much more
Than the last time
We made love.

And I call you
Lovely.
Because you are like love,
Always different, and
Always the same.
Sometimes in the very same bed
Where you can lie
Full and warm and content,
First you must feel
The bedsheets burn
From your tossing
In the lonely cold.

Eventually I will learn
Better names for you.
But until then, I won't ask
Your forgiveness for these.

At least they're
Beginning-of-the-sentence
Ways
Of saying
"I love you."

lady ice and eve

It's fun to fasten
Cork boards on our minds,
And toss little joke darts
At each other,
Carefully standing
Far enough apart
So that no stinging point
Has force enough
To crack the shield.

The competition is keen with you.
Your mind is quick,
And your darts are sharp.
But you don't really like
To stay across the room from me too long.
And sometimes you drop your shield
Unexpectedly soon,
To be next to me again.
And my last dart finds
A softer mark.

Then,
For all the pleasure of the game,
We both wish we'd never played.
Sometimes
You just laugh it off,
Because you know
How I shrink inside
When I hurt you.
That's when you decide
To learn a little toughness,
A little "cool" ...
To become a bit like
"Lady Ice."

"Lady Ice" walks tall,
With stern upswept hair ...
With ballet precision,
Around and between
Small dirty children,
Men,
And dogs.
Her smile

Is just an underline for her eyes.
"So much," they say,
"And not one bit more."
Her clothes are shaped by fashion,
Not by her body ...
Even when she walks the beach
Nearly nude.

Her lovers freeze
In her disdainful shadow.
From her crayon lips,
Love words sound
Almost lewd.
She twists
Her silken scarf around life,
Choking hopes
With firm demands.
Turning diamonds into ice.

Don't be "Lady Ice."

Stay instead
A tropic ocean,
Rolling with me in your warm waves.
Ice is hard,
You are as soft and supple
As a baby's tongue,
Pressing against me.
Those who don't understand our game
Call you cold enough,
For only I
May share your bed.

"Lady Ice"?
She's easy enough to name.
But I have no name enough for you.
You are too close.

You are the hair
I feel on my neck ...
The salty net of perspiration
Between us ...
Is it yours, or mine ...
It doesn't matter.
And who can tell.

A name is a word ...
Too stubby and unlovely
To describe what you are
With me.

Perhaps I'll call you Eve someday ...
Because I think Adam's first sin
Was in her excitement.
He had all he needed to be a happy man,
But she offered him
A taste of more,
In a way
He didn't understand.

Pretend a harder crust
If you must,
But make it hard candy
Instead of ice.
Then you can be
The caramel candy-coated apple carrier
For me.
And all through life ...
I'll bite.

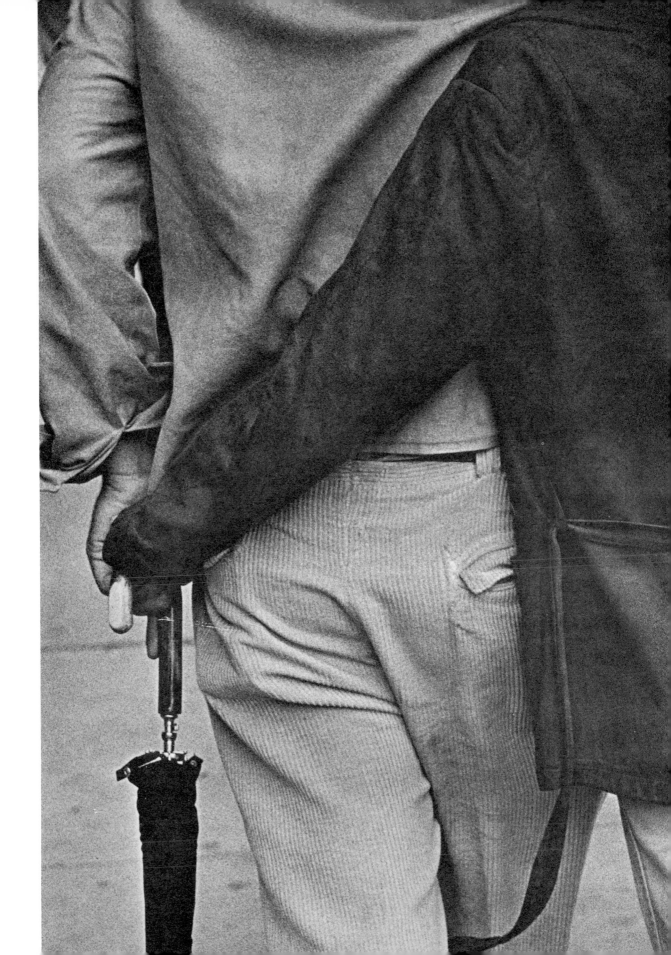

Watch the way people walk.
It shows how they live.
Stumblers, ploughing the ground
With their eyes
See only mud and sidewalks,
Feet and ankles.
That's why mountaintops and jet planes
And the soft bouncing of passing girls
Are missing from their lives.

The pavement pounders strut and push.
They don't seem to care that it's unlucky
To step on cracks in the sidewalk,
Or on people who get in their way.
They never find lucky pennies,
Or taste the flavor of the week
From the pushcart ice cream man.

Men who walk with their hands in their pockets
Have something to hide.
Women, slouching along on their heels,

walking

Haven't felt pretty in such a long time
They don't care anymore.

When a man and woman aren't easy with each other
Her hands show too many knuckles
She should be holding his arm
Or hiding in his hand.
And his smile gets very thin
If he makes her run
To keep up with him.

We walk together beautifully.
You take a step and a half
For every one of mine.
But we stay together easily.
You hold my arm like dancing,
My elbow brushing your breast,
Your hips moving by my leg.

I've been walking very tall
Since you've been walking by my side.

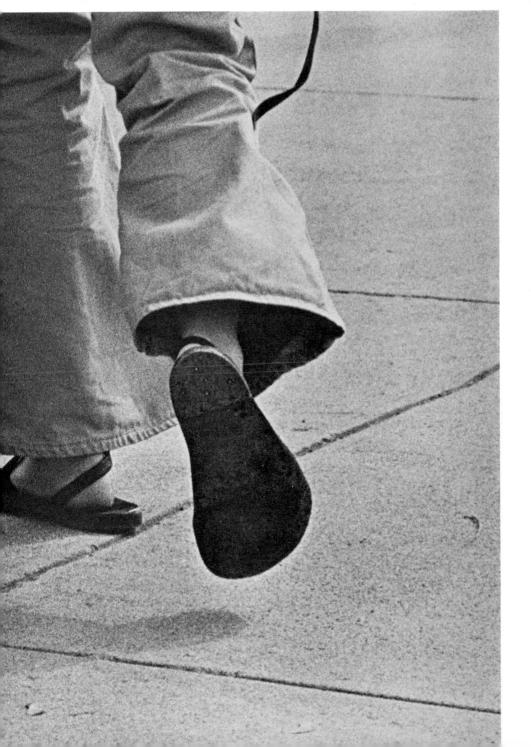

your innocence

If I spent as much time
Watching you as I'd like to,
I'd bump into chairs and tables,
And cars in parking lots.
It isn't that I don't believe
The way your curves tumble
When you skip down the stairs,
Or bounce out of a car.
But I must admit
I never thought I'd get to see
Anything quite like you.
That's why I can't really blame other men
When their greed for you
Shows in their eyes.

You don't appetize them on purpose.
In fact you don't even notice
The older ones,
Trying to flatten out their pot bellies,
And puffing up their chests ...
Or the younger ones,
Deepening their voices,
And looking hard into your eyes.

You don't believe you do that to men.
It's as if you thought you were
In some kind of a crowd,
And someone behind you
Was causing all the commotion,
Someday I'll get through to you.
I'll make you understand
How it really is.

You're so much woman,
That when you are in a room,
You use up all the curved space that's there.

A woman is supposed to make soft
Wherever she goes.
But you make all the soft
That any room can hold.
There's no space left
For one other woman,

Let alone some crowd.
That's why men think
You're playing games with them.
They expect you to appreciate yourself.
And you don't,
Even after you've been surprised and hurt,
At least twice that I know of.
How can I help you live safe
In your soft sweater innocence,
In this man jungle.
I don't want animal breath
Burning your skin.
Hey ...
Am I being honest?
Or just jealous.
I hate to see you even give another man
One of your eye-smiles.

Come ... now.
Gather all that womanliness of yours
Into your lap.
Curl around it,
And keep it purring kitten warm,
Until I come and wrap myself in you again ...
And distract you
With talk of hair,
And war,
And rain again today ...
While my fingers gently climb
The scented nylon walls you wear.

Or am I distracting you?
Your smile always seems to get gentler
As your shoulders
Feel warmer.

You can flood me,
With just as much of you as I can hold
Between my thumb and forefinger ...
Or between my lips.

Touch here ...
Where my lips are on you ...
With your palm ... touch
And feel your grace and beauty with me.
Know you are safe.
Then I'll know
You're mine.

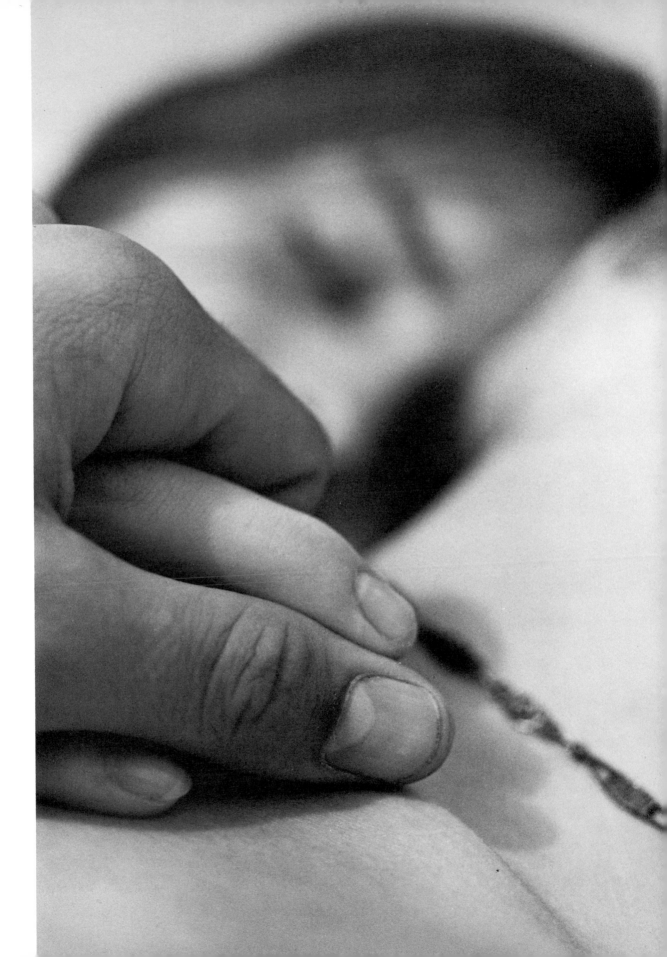

closer

Now,
While your arms lie
On top of mine
You say your hands belong to me.
But they don't really.
I can't tickle myself with my hands.
But you make ripples of my ribs with yours.

And certainly your eyes are not mine.
They see me as splendid.
In fact, you have stranger's eyes.
They're never twice the same.

When you open them to me
I suddenly can't swallow
The brassy taste
Of a large smooth shining coin
On the sides of my tongue.

How can we be strangers
When we've warmed
In so many dawns together.
I've stood and watched in the mirror
So next to you
That I was breathing the shreds
Of brown brushings from your hair,
An aroma like rain drops
Splashing in summer dust.
I remember melting night words
On the warm of your neck
Lying against my cheek ...
While those fingers of "ours"
Were lifting and bundling your hair
With a pink elastic band.

For all the times I've
Smeared your lipstick,
Trying to catch your tongue
While it was still running rebel red into smiles,
Your lips always taste the way
I think a stranger's would.

You are different
Every time we make love.
And you change me so much each time

That I'm jealous
Of the men I was before.
Jealousy is a spear.
But mine never hurts you,
Because you dissolve it
In the grinding cream
That you call
"Just your love."

But I want to know
Before I hold your hand
How your wrists will feel
Pulsing on mine.
Even as my fingers
Fill the spaces between yours
I can't really touch you
Through this hot sheet metal
Flexing just under my skin.

Are you
Pony muzzle soft
Where your body breathes your soul?
I don't know.
And I would if we were really one.

Watch the clock
Draw ever tightening circles
Of the minutes passing around us.
When our hour is counted,
We will be crushed in death.
But still, not together.
Because first the softer ,
Then the tougher of us
Will feel life's minute circle
Tighten to a period.

If we are ever to be together,
It must be now.

Tighten with me
As closely as a rhyme.
Taste the last lemon
Of my loneliness.

Now, mix with me here,
In the red, warm dark
Of your mouth.

tears

When you were a little girl,
Little sadnesses
And scraped knees
Made you cry.
A doll's broken arm ...
A tumble from
A playground swing ...
A piece of candy
You had to wait
Until after lunch to eat ...
Little boys who pulled
Your pretty brown hair.

Then came days
Of secret tears,
Sometimes
For no reason.
Just tears,
In front of a mirror
In your room.
That's when songs
Began to make you cry,
And sad movies,
And thirty-five cent magazines,
With color pictures and stories
About singers and actors
And their sunny
Plastic-coated lives.

Wasn't there a horse in your life
Right about then?
I don't know
If you ever really rode him,
Or if you just liked to draw his picture
And pretend he carried you away,
Over golden fields,
Across deep surging rivers,
And under tall quiet trees.

And you cried
When slightly bigger boys
Threw snowballs at you,
And tried to tangle
Your first home-permanent hair.
That was about the time
When just the right kind of tears
Won your first high heels and lipstick.
And you had to learn
To walk and talk all over again.
And how could they
Pass over you for cheerleader then?
But they did.
And you cried
A little different kind of tear.
Your tears became subtler things,
Much gentler pink than your cheeks,
And very real.

You cried for hungry children,
Cold at Christmastime,
And a glance
That fell just short
Of a smile,
From someone
Whose eyes were very kind;
And over the hurts
A friend endured,
Because she had
A different color skin;
And the something more than curls
Between you
When you fixed your mother's hair,
And found
A little silver there;
And the end of school at graduation,
And the smash of death against someone
Who grew up with you.

But did you cry
When I first met you?
I wish I knew.

I know you cry
When the new green South Wind
Brushes your forehead,
As it clicks the castanets
Of early spring's
Sleet-sheathed branches.

And I've seen new planets
Tangle in your eyes
When the dancing moon excites you
As she sheds her last cloud veil,
And arches naked, full, and wanton
Against the purple, fur-lined sky.

But those were still different tears
My fingers found near your ears,
When I rested my head
On your shoulder,
And I felt the roses
Of your warm spring hills
Blossom on my neck.

In fact your whole body
Seemed to sob,
And your skin bore tears
No eyes could grow,
When I unfastened
That scarlet velvet ribbon,
And your warm
Dark brown hair
Tumbled its perfume
Around my face and arms.

You were a warm bubbling spring
Inside your lips.
And I drank you
Full,
And long,
And deep.

naked eyes

Do you know that
You're always looking down ...
Like you're hoping to find
Something you lost a long time ago.
Why not look at me
Because I'd like to get to know you.
Even when we're holding hands together,
You still look thin and lonely,
Like a curl of water
From a broken water tap.

I've tried to touch your love ...
Make it surge a little stronger,
Like pressing fingers on a nozzle
Makes a drinking fountain leap.
But I guess you don't feel my fingers;
Because even when you smile a little
I get the feeling that
Somehow you've gone asleep.

Are your eyes too naked
To lay them here on mine?
Come and let me touch
Your neck and shoulders,
Let my fingers paint
Your legs and arms with fire;
Hear my tongue pound rods of thunder
Shaped for you to ride.

My breath gets warmed and tangled
In your soft, fine, sun-streaked hair.
Your lips were shaped to suck
The wild sweaty juice from life.
No jar can hold
And keep this drink;
It's too hot,
It breaks the glass.

Carefully keep this spurting sauce,
For once spilled,
It dries and cakes so soon.
Now when you're young
And strong enough
How can I make you care,
And dare enough
To tilt your head,
Brush back your hair,
And lay your naked eyes
On mine.

the thin line

There's a very thin line
Between lovers and strangers.
Lovers grow their love
By feeding each other ... love.
Lovers depend on each other.
But strangers
Depend on strangers too.

There couldn't have been
A Beatles, or a Beethoven,
If no one bothered to listen.
Presidents and kings
Can scream bloody war at each other,
But no war can start
Until some private fires a gun.

I want to give you all that I am
And take all you have to give.
But strangers need a slice of us too.
And there are such things as friends.

There's a very thin line
Between lovers and strangers.
Any man may watch the way you move
As you walk down the street,
And smile if your sweater
Is just a little tight.
But your breasts are
My
Pillows.
The only place I can find
Soft enough
For me to rest my aching head.

Just thinking how you feel
Soothes my smashed up mind.
But strangers think too ...
Sometimes the same thoughts
That lovers do.

And I've seen you stand
Close enough to someone else
For him to breathe the autumn scent
Of your freshly shampooed hair.
He must wish
For our laughing,
Soap-rubbing showers
Just like I do.

There's a very thin line
Between lovers and strangers.
We live together
Not because we're afraid
Of living alone,
But because it's so good
Living together.

If you cry from slicing onions,
Or because you don't feel loved enough today,
I can brush the tear away
Carefully
So I won't scratch your cheek
With my day's end beard,
And slice the onion for you.
When I do,
You make me feel like
King Arthur,
Cutting off the ear
Of the onion dragon,
Or like Merlin the Magician,
Changing a teary little girl
Into his furry, fiery woman ...
You only have to open
For my kiss.

A stranger
Could
Slice that onion.
And a friend
Could
Brush away that tear.
How often would he have to do it
Until it felt the same as me.
How often would you have to let him
Until it felt the same as us.

There's a very thin line
Between lovers and strangers.
Dawn surprises the middle of the night.
And "yes" many times begins with "no."

Draw that thin line.
Keep strangers
At the outer edges of your perfume.
Ignore the heavy eyes
They put on you
When you walk.
Listen to friends' ideas,
But not breathlessly and
Starry-eyed.
Laugh at their jokes,
But not helplessly.

Remember,
The outline of your body
Against bed sheets
Is much too full and lovely and round
To be the thin line
Between lovers and strangers.

I need you too much.

we take each other too much for granted

We take each other too much for granted.
Yes, even us.
I know we said we never would.
But look how far apart
We stand when we talk.
Why not stand
Very close beside me
All the time.
That way I can enjoy
Inhaling the freshness
Of your hair.
It's like the scent
Of the few grains
Of freshly ground coffee
That sometimes stick to a spoon ...
And it's especially delicious
Mixed with the milky scent of your body
As you first step out of a soapy shower.
And your neck really is warmer
Under your hair,
Than at your throat, you know.
But I can only feel the difference
With my cheek.

We take each other too much for granted.
Even though we said we never would.
I've kissed you thousands of times.
So why should it take
Putting my fingers
Here on your lips like this
To feel which of your lips
Is softer ...
And how gently they part.
I never knew your kisses were that moist.
Why didn't you tell me you like
The taste of fingertips.

Just think,
You won't have to buy lipstick.
From now on,
I'll rub your lips pink,

And please my fingers
At the same time.

I never even touched your ears before,
Although I'm sure
You would have let me.
The edges of your ears
Are almost as soft
As your lips.
And your earlobes are even softer.

Let's never take each other
So much for granted anymore.
Let's see how long
And how deep
I can look into your eyes.
Now I can see them change color.
And they seem to get wider
The longer I look.

Just because you and I are for keeps
Let's never take the chance
That our bodies might get so far apart
That the distance could get in the way
Of getting ourselves
Closer together.

I love to touch your hands.
Not just your fingers
But your wrists too ...
And just around the edges
Of your fingernails.
I've noticed that your eyes
Can get almost as moist as your lips
When I touch the creases of your palms.

That's like putting my love
Into your hands,
And feeling you clasp your fingers
Very tight.

Your fingers just warmed my mind.
Was it growing cold?
I didn't think so.
But let's not
Take each other for granted
Anymore.

quiet

When you walk with me
You have a certain sound.
Your legs are exclamation points,
Your spike heels dot the ground.
You're a wrestling nylon swirl.
A jingling chain around your neck
Holds a dangling pendant set with pearl.
Your hopping, skipping laugh escapes
From stretching hidden snapping straps.
And when you cry, tears tingle down
Like a drinking kitten's thirsty laps.

And that was you, until tonight.
Tonight,
I saw you move on velvet by his side.
You made a quiet together
That was more than just no noise.
Your voice was chilled satin
That unfolded in words
That covered my ears.
Your unstockinged legs
Flexed gently from your toes
To your hips.

You flowed around his arm,
No nylon swirl, no snapping straps,
No jingling pendant chain
Could pry apart the quiet
As you grew together.
It's cousin to the quiet
That I've heard
Under ancient pines at sunrise,
And in the space between
A sleeping newborn baby's breaths.

I understand that quiet,
Maybe better than you do.

It happens when you're comfortable
Though you don't have words to say.
It happens when you fall in love,
When you fall in love to stay.

Sounds and words are things for now
But quiet came before them both.
And when the sounds and words are gone,
Quiet will seal mankind's last oath.

Walk with me now.
Make lots of sound.
Jingle your chain.
Dot your heels on the ground.

It's time for noise.
Clown, drink, and sing.
Kill the damned quiet
Your hand could bring.

The incredible quiet
Your hand could bring
If you were wearing
My golden ring.

. . .The world should know how warm
Two hands in one coat pocket feel
On a cold night,
Or how a cool and gentle hand can soothe
All the anger from a fist.

But I'm glad no one can overhear
Our long, private
Finger — conversations . . . .

lovin touch
dick summer